ideals
NEIGHBORLY ISSUE

Just let me be a neighbor kind
To all who pass my door;
Then may I travel paths to find
Oh, just so many more.

May I but lend my hands to help
Those who are in much need,
With a regard not for myself,
But for those who might heed.

May I speak words of kindness, too,
And watch them grow to be
A channel where returns come through
To cheer the heart of me.

Leisetta Brodt

Editorial Director, James Kuse
Managing Editor, Ralph Luedtke
Associate Editor, Robin Lee Dennison
Photographic Editor, Gerald Koser
Production Editor, Stuart L. Zyduck

Dear, Lovely Summer

Dear, lovely summer,
I do envy you
With sunshine and cloud dreams
And skies bright and blue,
The little ones happy
With school at an end,
And each day so precious
With beauties to lend.

Dear, lovely summer,
When trees reach to God
With green leaves and blossoms
And earth's growing sod;
How fresh is the morning,
How pleasant the noon,
The quiet of evening
With heaven in tune.

Dear, golden summer,
My heart holds it all:
The sound of the cricket,
The redbird's glad call,
The stream in the valley
That ambles along,
The laughter of children,
The splendor of song.

Bright, smiling summer,
With green hills to climb,
All beauties of nature
I proudly call mine,
The sweet hours of dreaming
With nothing to do,
Dear, lovely summer,
Oh, yes, I love you.

Garnett Ann Schultz

IDEALS—Vol. 35, No. 3—May 1978. Published bimonthly by IDEALS PUBLISHING CORPORATION, 11315 Watertown Plank Road, Milwaukee, Wis. 53226. Second-class postage paid at Milwaukee, Wisconsin. © 1978 by IDEALS PUBLISHING CORPORATION. All rights reserved. Title IDEALS registered U.S. Patent Office.

ONE YEAR SUBSCRIPTION—six consecutive issues as published—only $10.00
TWO YEAR SUBSCRIPTION—twelve consecutive issues as published—only $17.00
SINGLE ISSUES—only $2.50

ISBN 0-89542-314-6

Photograph opposite
MT. WASHINGTON
NEW HAMPSHIRE
Fred Sieb

Neighborly Gifts

It may be just a friendly wave,
Or maybe a hello,
Or just a talk across the fence
As neighbors do, you know.

For it can lighten up the heart
And bring a happy smile,
To have a neighbor for a friend
And make the day worthwhile.

A chore can be much lighter
When a neighbor helps you lift;
And the friendships of a lifetime
Are a rare and precious gift.

My earthly treasures are the kind
It's nice to give away:
A smile, a nod, a warm hello,
From my neighbor across the way.

Mildred L. Jarrell

My Neighbor's Clothesline

There are sheets and pillowcases
  And a dozen towels or so,
And little dresses blowing out
  Like flowers in a row.
A tablecloth, a baby's shawl,
  A quilt hung out to air,
And looking at her line I see
  A hundred stories there.

I know she loves her beds to be
  As fresh as April skies,
The dresses for her little girl
  Are blue to match her eyes.
The tablecloth has little sprigs
  Of daisies 'broidered on,
As if she plucked the tiny ones
  That grew about the lawn.

Her aprons are so bright and gay,
  I know she loves to cook;
She makes a game of everything
  Like people in a book.
And so her clothesline is to me
  A kind of study chart,
That tells me all the lovely things
  She dreams within her heart.

Edna Jaques

The House by the Side of the Road

There are hermit souls that live withdrawn
    In the peace of their self-content;
There are souls, like stars, that dwell apart
    In a fellowless firmament;

There are pioneer souls that blaze their paths
    Where highways never ran;
But let me live by the side of the road
    And be a friend to man.

Let me live in a house by the side of the road,
    Where the race of men go by—
The men who are good and the men who are bad,
    As good and as bad as I;
I would not sit in the scorner's seat,
    Or hurl the cynic's ban;
Let me live in a house by the side of the road
    And be a friend to man.

I see from my house by the side of the road,
    By the side of the highway of life,
The men who press with the ardor of hope,
    The men who are faint with the strife.
But I turn not away from their smiles nor their tears—
    Both parts of an infinite plan;
Let me live in my house by the side of the road
    And be a friend to man.

I know there are brook-gladdened meadows ahead,
    And mountains of wearisome height,
That the road passes on through the long afternoon
    And stretches away to the night.
But still I rejoice when the travelers rejoice
    And weep with the strangers that moan,
Nor live in my house by the side of the road
    Like a man who dwells alone.

Let me live in my house by the side of the road
    Where the race of men go by—
They are good, they are bad, they are weak, they are strong,
    Wise, foolish—so am I.
Then why should I sit in the scorner's seat
    Or hurl the cynic's ban?
Let me live in my house by the side of the road
    And be a friend to man.

Sam Walter Foss

Edgar A. Guest

For over fifty years, Americans began their day with coffee, the newspaper and a "Breakfast Table Chat" with Edgar A. Guest. Each day brought a new verse on subjects common to all: home, mothers, a simple religious faith, and hard work. This personification of the American dream was born in Birmingham, England, in 1881 and came with his parents to Detroit at the age of ten. Guest left high school after one year to financially help his family. He had a series of minor jobs, ending as a newspaper sportswriter. There, he found that he had a talent for writing verse which touched the hearts of his readers. Until his death in 1959, he wrote a poem a day for publication. At the height of his popularity, his column was syndicated in over 300 newspapers; and he estimated that he had written over 10,000 poems. Never praised by literary critics, Guest, nevertheless, brought pleasure to millions who believed in the same decent and honorable values as did he.

How to Feel Better

Want to feel better? I'll give you
  the way:
That task you've neglected, get at
  it today!
That letter unwritten, that visit
  unpaid,
That failure to keep to a promise
  you made;
Get at them this minute and clear
  off your mind
And very much better you'll feel
  you will find.

Want to feel better? I'll tell you
  just how
You can sit back in comfort a few
  hours from now
And glow with contentment and
  genuine pride,
Get rid of those duties which
  you've shoved aside.
Just clear off the desk of your
  mind once again
And you'll walk with the step of
  all light-hearted men.

Want to feel better? Go out of
  your way
To someone who's lonely; and do
  it today!
Forget the excuses so easy to find,
Get your heart lighter and clear
  off your mind.
Get free from regret which a
  death might reveal
And you'll be surprised how
  much better you'll feel.

Neighborly

Not great, but neighborly I'd be,
With eyes that are awake to see
The tender little lines of care
Upon the faces everywhere—
With wisdom that can understand
From just the pressure of a hand,
Or just a word, voiced soft and low,
Whether the heart be glad or no.

Along my little path I ask
Full strength to meet my daily task,
And then this knowledge: that there beat
No truer hearts than those I meet;
That all that life has power to give
Lies round about me where I live;
That rich or poor, unto the end,
Or high or low, a friend's a friend!

Not far I'd travel. There's no need!
Here I can do the kindly deed.
Here I can laugh and live and learn.
Here all the lights as brightly burn
As those which shine on haunts afar.
Here troops of merry children are,
Grown men and women good to know,
What more can distant scenes bestow?

Not great, but neighborly I'd be.
Would better know the ones I see
From day to day, and better share
Their fleeting joys and times of care.
I'd speak with deeper meaning, too,
The morning's greeting: "How d'you do!"
And reap from life as much of love
As those who reach the heights above.

The Kindly Neighbor

I have a kindly neighbor, one who stands
Beside my gate and chats with me awhile,
Gives me the glory of his radiant smile
And comes at times to help with willing hands.
No station high or rank this man commands;
He, too, must trudge, as I, the long day's mile;
And yet, devoid of pomp or gaudy style,
He has a worth exceeding stocks or lands.
To him I go when sorrow's at my door;
On him I lean when burdens come my way;
Together oft we talk our trials o'er,
And there is warmth in each good night we say.
A kindly neighbor! Wars and strife shall end
When man has made the man next door his friend.

May Basket

Wallpaper, scissors, and flour paste
   To greet the month of May—
Let's slip along a backward path
   And shrug the years away!

The older children cut and shaped
   Each gay-sprigged paper cone;
The youngest maybe stood and gaped
   Or tried to shape its own.

Then, knowing every woodland haunt,
   We crawled on briar-scratched knees
To pick spring beauties, violets,
   And frail anemones,

Or lady slippers, wildwood fern,
   And kitten breeches, too;
Sweet Williams, heavy on their stems,
   And fresh as morning dew.

The paper cones were flower filled,
And paper handles dried;
Then down the dusty road we trudged,
   Arms loaded, side by side.

No greater pleasure have I known,
   Nor would I dare to ask it,
Than knocking on each friendly door
   And calling out "May basket!"

Esther Ken Thomas

Photograph opposite
MAY BASKETS
Gerald Koser

My Mother

Who fed me from her gentle breast,
And hush'd me in her arms to rest,
And on my cheeks sweet kisses prest?
    My Mother.

When sleep forsook my open eye,
Who was it sang sweet hushaby
And rock'd me that I should not cry?
    My Mother.

Who sat and watched my infant head,
When sleeping on my cradle bed,
And tears of sweet affection shed?
    My Mother.

When pain and sickness made me cry,
Who gaz'd upon my heavy eye,
And wept, for fear that I should die?
    My Mother.

Who drest my doll in clothes so gay,
And taught me pretty how to play,
And minded all I had to say?
    My Mother.

Who ran to help me when I fell,
And would some pretty story tell,
Or kiss the place to make it well?
    My Mother.

Who taught my infant lips to pray,
And love God's holy book and day,
And walk in wisdom's pleasant way?
    My Mother.

And can I ever cease to be
Affectionate and kind to thee,
Who wast so very kind to me,
    My Mother.

Ah! no, the thought I cannot bear,
And if God please my life to spare,
I hope I shall reward thy care,
    My Mother.

When thou art feeble, old, and gray,
My healthy arm shall be thy stay,
And I will soothe thy pains away,
    My Mother.

And when I see thee hang thy head,
'Twill be my turn to watch thy bed,
And tears of sweet affection shed,
    My Mother.

For God Who lives above the skies,
Would look with vengeance in His eyes,
If I should ever dare despise
    My Mother.

Ann Taylor

When Little Feet Wander

When little feet wander,
Where do they go?
Along a bright pathway
Of flowers that grow

Close to a wishing well,
Lost in the shade,
Where fairy folk gather
And wishes are made.

When little feet travel,
They skip here and there
As lightly as if
They are walking on air;

They wade in the coolness
Where silver brooks run
And dry their brown toes
In gold patches of sun.

Whenever they journey,
No matter how far,
You know they'll be coming
Back home where you are;

For little feet tire
Of trudging along
And end up in bed
Where they rightly belong.

Marguerite Gode

*Photograph opposite
Vivienne*

Thoughts on Friendship

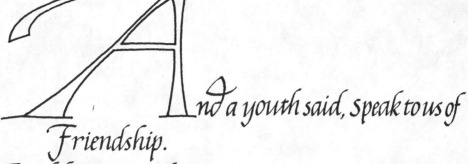And a youth said, Speak to us of
Friendship.
And he answered, saying:
Your friend is your needs answered.
He is your field which you sow with love and reap with
thanksgiving.
And he is your board and your fireside.
For you come to him with your hunger, and you seek
him for peace.

When your friend speaks his mind you fear not the
"nay" in your own mind, nor do you withhold
the "ay."
And when he is silent your heart ceases not to listen to
his heart;
For without words, in friendship, all thoughts, all
desires, all expectations are born and shared,
with joy that is unacclaimed.
When you part from your friend, you grieve not;

Kahlil Gibran

For that which you love most in him may be clearer
     in his absence, as the mountain to the climber is
     clearer from the plain.

And let there be no purpose in friendship save the
     deepening of the spirit.

For love that seeks aught but the disclosure of its own
     mystery is not love but a net cast forth: and
     only the unprofitable is caught.

And let your best be for your friend.

If he must know the ebb of your tide, let him know
     its flood also.

For what is your friend that you should seek him with
     hours to kill?

Seek him always with hours to live.

For it is his to fill your need, but not your emptiness.

And in the sweetness of friendship let there be laugh=
     ter, and sharing of pleasures.

For in the dew of little things the heart finds its
     morning and is refreshed.

Scribe: Abraham Lincoln

A Country Place

The country is a friendly place;
You'll find a smile on every face,
A welcome greeting, bright hello,
The kind of folks you'd love to know.
'Tis different when you visit here,
For country folks are warm, sincere.

The country is a field of green,
A blue sky and a flowing stream,
A farmhouse and a winding lane
Where surely you shall come again,
An invitation from the heart,
A welcome handshake from the start.

The country is quite quaint and small,
Sophistication not at all;
For friendliness is always there
If skies are dull, if skies are fair,
A happiness, a smiling face;
God dwells within a country place.

Garnett Ann Schultz

Photograph opposite
BARNETT, VERMONT
Richard W. Brown

Your Neighbor

Do you know the neighbor who lives in your block;
Do you ever take time for a bit of a talk?
Do you know his troubles, his heartaches, his cares,
The battles he's fighting, the burdens he bears?
Do you greet him with joy or pass him right by
With a questioning look and a quizzical eye?

Do you bid him "Good morning" and "How do you do,"
Or shrug up as if he were nothing to you?
He may be a chap with a mighty big heart
And a welcome that grips, if you just do your part.
And I know you'll coax out his sunniest smile
If you'll stop with this neighbor and visit awhile.

We rush on so fast in these strenuous days;
We're apt to find fault when it's better to praise.
We judge a man's worth by the make of his car;
We're anxious to find what his politics are.
But somehow it seldom gets under the hide,
The fact that the fellow we're living beside

Is a fellow like us, with a hankering, too,
For a grip of the hand and a "How do you do!"
With a heart that responds in a welcome sincere
If you'll just stop to fling him a message of cheer;
And I know you'll coax out his sunniest smile
If you'll stop with this neighbor and visit awhile.

H. Howard Biggar

To My Friend

I have never been rich before,
  But you have poured
Into my heart's high door
  A golden hoard.

My wealth is the vision shared,
  The sympathy,
The feast of the soul prepared
  By you for me.

Together we wander through
  The wooded ways,
Old beauties are green and new
  Seen through your gaze.

I look for no greater prize
  Than your soft voice.
The steadiness of your eyes
  Is my heart's choice.

I have never been rich before,
  But I divine
Your step on my sunlit floor
  And wealth is mine!

Anne Campbell

Friends

If all the sorrows of this weary earth—
  The pains and heartaches of humanity—
  If all were gathered up and given me,

I still would have my share of wealth and worth
  Who have you, Friend of Old, to be my cheer
  Through life's uncertain fortunes, year by year.

Thank God for friends, who dearer grow as years increase:
  Who, as possessions fail our hopes and hands,
  Become the boon supreme, than gold and lands

More precious. Let all else, if must be, cease;
  But, Lord of Life, I pray on me bestow
  The gift of friends, to share the way I go.

Thomas Curtis Clark

Blessed Are They

Blessed are they who are pleasant to live with—
Blessed are they who sing in the morning;
Whose faces have smiles for their early adorning;
Who come down to breakfast companioned by cheer;
Who don't dwell on troubles or entertain fear;
Whose eyes smile forth bravely; whose lips curve to say:
"Life, I salute you! Good morrow, new day!"
Blessed are they who are pleasant to live with—
Blessed are they who treat one another,
Though merely a sister, a father or brother,
With the very same courtesy they would extend
To a casual acquaintance or dearly loved friend;
Who choose for the telling encouraging things;
Who choke back the bitter, the sharp word that stings;
Who bestow love on others throughout the long day—
Pleasant to live with and blessed are they.

Wilhelmina Stitch

A Smile

A smile costs nothing but gives much—
It takes but a moment, but the memory of it usually
    lasts forever.
None are so rich that can get along without it—
And none are so poor but that can be made rich by it.
It enriches those who receive
Without making poor those who give.
It creates sunshine in the home,
Fosters goodwill in business
And is the best antidote for trouble.
It cannot be begged, borrowed or stolen; for
    it is of no value
Unless it is freely given away.
Some people are too busy to give you a smile;
Give them one of yours,
For the good Lord knows that no one needs a
    smile so badly
As he or she who has no more smiles left to give.

Author Unknown

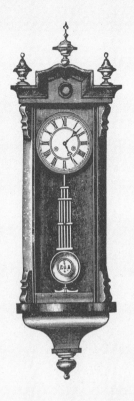

COUNTRY AUCTION

Go to a country auction,
And there I'm sure you'll find
All types of people waiting
In one accorded mind.

Both city folk and farmer
Will sit there in the sun,
For hours and hours unended,
To bid and have some fun.

There'll be beds, chairs and blankets,
Oil lamps and bric-a-brac;
There'll be bureaus, chests and organs,
And patchwork quilts all tacked.

There'll be pots, pans and dishes,
Hayrakes and oxen yoke,
Baskets filled with odds and ends
To make them laugh and joke.

There'll be books, iron kettles,
And parlor stoves, a few,
Radios, chambers, cowbells,
And tables all askew.

There'll be candlesticks of silver,
Old saws and handmade nails;
Cut-glass vases, braided rugs
And even milking pails.

Visit a country auction,
And you will get a thrill
If you just sit and watch them
And not your wagon fill!

Gertrude Rudberg

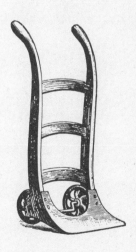

Photograph opposite
John H. Vondell

BOX SUPPER SOCIALS

"If the girl was worth it, we'd bid all the way up to 75¢ just for the privilege of eating her box supper. That's not so high, considering you also got the girl for the evening, too."

My husband and a favorite brother-in-law were reminiscing about those joyful evenings back in the 1920s and '30s when the box-supper social was popular.

Every town had its matchmaker— "remember Freddie Glau's wife, Clara?"—and she usually organized the socials. "Even though I was only making about $12 a week," Walt recalled, "I figured it was a good investment. I got a fine meal, a dancing partner, and the chance to take her home—all for less than a dollar!"

The young ladies arose early and spent the day in the kitchen, mixing, chopping, cooking, baking and fussing so they could fill a shoebox or basket with tempting morsels. Fried chicken, homemade crock pickles, blueberry muffins, poppy seed cake were all prettily packed and beribboned with one goal in mind: the highest bid from the boy their cook hoped would become a beau.

Many a time, my husband remembers, "coercion and corruption were rampant at bidding time, and a fellow had to be very discreet." Some of the best cooks in town were not necessarily—well, shall we say the "best looking" girls around—and some of the other good cooks had seven left feet when it came to dancing. A man had to use caution to make sure the right bid went with the right box. Husbands had better make sure they were the highest bidders for their wives' boxes—"or else!"—and there was always the free-loading type who wouldn't bid but wanted to share in the spoils.

The highest bidder not only established a young lady's popularity, but he earned the right to enjoy a summer night in the park with his lass by his side while they shared the homemade feast. After supper, "somebody always made some kind of patriotic speech before the dancing began," Walt said. Then it was right into the high-spirited tempo of a polka or a schottische, a circle two-step or a square dance. "And, for some reason," my husband recalled, "the caller was always named Curley."

The box-supper social was something like a blind date. "If you had your cap set for some pretty little thing, the social was a perfect chance to get to know her. Even your folks approved."

Like many another gentle American custom, the box-supper social is pretty much a thing of the past. Precooked chicken in a plastic bucket may be quick and filling, but it can never replace the laughter and companionship that so long ago were packed, along with the pickles, into a box supper.

Bea Bourgeois

John H. Vondell

 Daisies have a heart of gold;
I guess that must be why
They grow profusely everywhere
In fields that meet the sky.

Dorothy Butler Kimball

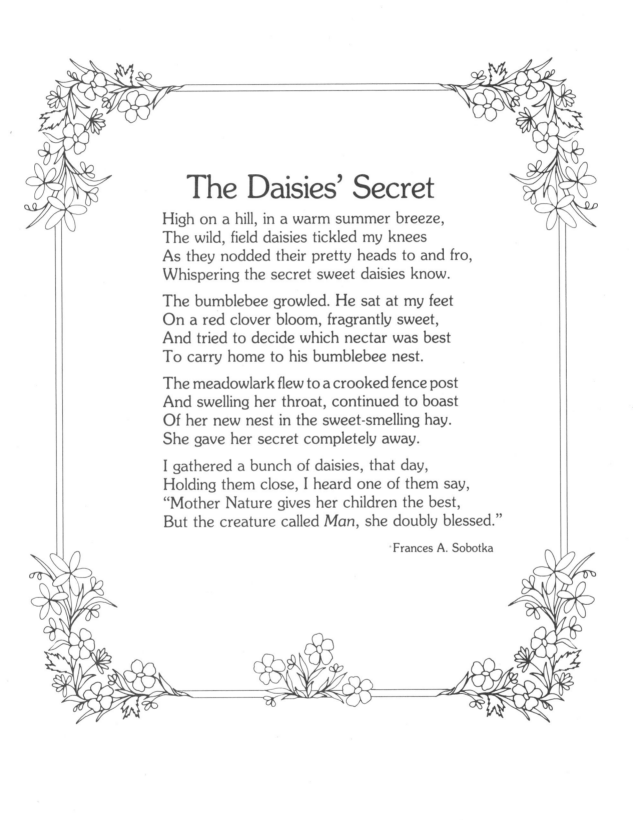

The Daisies' Secret

High on a hill, in a warm summer breeze,
The wild, field daisies tickled my knees
As they nodded their pretty heads to and fro,
Whispering the secret sweet daisies know.

The bumblebee growled. He sat at my feet
On a red clover bloom, fragrantly sweet,
And tried to decide which nectar was best
To carry home to his bumblebee nest.

The meadowlark flew to a crooked fence post
And swelling her throat, continued to boast
Of her new nest in the sweet-smelling hay.
She gave her secret completely away.

I gathered a bunch of daisies, that day,
Holding them close, I heard one of them say,
"Mother Nature gives her children the best,
But the creature called *Man*, she doubly blessed."

Frances A. Sobotka

Summer Showers

Silver web of water
On the window glass,
Crystal droplets clinging
To the emerald grass,

Pungent smell of thirsty earth
Soaking moisture up,
Pastel blossom chalices
Brimming like a cup,

Rainbow-hued umbrellas
Above the folks you meet,
Children wading puddles
Up and down the street,

The patter as of tiny hooves
On leaf and roof and pane,
What pleasant things accompany
God's gift of summer rain!

Virginia Blanck Moore

Summer Rain

I love the sound of falling rain
Upon a tranquil summer day.
Thin silver chimes on my thatched roof
Ring out in such a magic way.

The flowers greet the rain with joy
And raise their heads when day is done.
They know the rain is their good friend
And offer thanks in unison.

The little meadow pools are starred
With silver ripples by the rain;
The hermit thrush sends forth its song
Because the earth is fresh again.

The old earth has such lovely things:
Warm sun and wind soft as a chime.
But there is nothing sweet as rain
Whose music is as old as time.

William Arnette Wofford

The Green World

Green blow the branches that hide my young,
Green are the boughs where my mate has sung;
Green leafy world of the summer's heart,
Holding my nest like a jewel apart;
And in the rustle of soft green shade,
This is a palace I would not trade;
This is the haven most loved I prize,
Safe from the peering of countless eyes.

Green arch the branches laced white with bloom,
Blackberry briars, sharing elbow room;
Wild rose blushing along the lane,
Theirs the contentment of sun and rain.
Come, songbirds, warble to heaven your praise,
Gladden the passer and bless his days!
Trill to the green world, sing to the dell,
"God's hand is over us—all is well!"

Louise Weibert Sutton

Picnicking as Before

The sun rose on a morning fair;
    The world was warm and sweet;
We packed a lunch and started for
    Our favorite retreat.

Our hearts were light as feathers, gay,
    That floated on the air;
And everything to us seemed right;
    The day was more than fair.

The birds were singing in the trees;
    The breeze was playful, gay.
And we sang as we rode along
    Where tall trees lined the way.

Remember all the fish we caught,
    The hours by the stream,
Our picnic neath the shady trees
    Where we could sit and dream?

Oh, I'll be glad when summer comes,
    And we can live once more
The happy, carefree hours we knew
    Picnicking as before.

Vera Laurel Hoffman

Fanfare

The fan is best known as a breeze maker. Long before our push-button age, fans were manipulated by hand and not objects of art or vanity. Instead, the fan was designed for practical purposes. As old as civilization, fans were first used to fan a spark into fire, drive away insects, winnow grain, and later prominent in religious ceremonies and processions.

According to legend, the use of the fan originated in China. The daughter of the mandarin became very warm at the Feast of the Lanterns, removed her mask and began fanning herself with it. Other ladies followed her example; and the fan was born.

The fan came to the Western world by the old trade routes of the sea. It made its appearance in England during the reign of Richard II. Queen Elizabeth I became known as the patron of fans and owned a huge collection of them. In Shakespeare's time, no lady went forth in public without her fan; and gentlemen also used them. Kings and gentlemen of rank and fashion carried them where they went. In eighteenth-century England, men's fans were often as elaborate as the ladies'. One handed down to us as the definitive in gentlemen's fans is a folding, compact type, easily carried in the vest pocket, which opens into a circle and refolds between two sticks. Victorian fans were larger in size and Queen Victoria was often portrayed holding such a one, lavish and beautiful.

In America in the late 1790s, the Shakers of Harvard, Massachusetts, famous for their chair industry and medicinal herbs, also made fans. These were of turkey feathers and sometimes decorated with peacock eyes and rosettes. It is believed they learned their fan making from the Indians of the Nashaway Valley.

The fans of later eras remained beautiful, fanciful, and suited to the whims in fashion. Through the years, fans have been fashioned of many materials: the ribs, or sticks, of ivory, sandalwood, jade, mother of pearl, leather, fruitwood, ebony, and Goodyear rubber, to mention only a few. The more expensive ones had sticks inlaid with silver, gold, and jewels; carving and piercing were also popular. The body of the fan was comprised of many fabrics, such as silk, satin, rare lace, gauze, parchment, silver foil, feathers and many other materials. Peacock feathers and ostrich plumes were also popular materials. In addition, fans have been encrusted with gems, embroidery, sequins and lavish designs defying description.

Fans have been designed for many purposes —with peepholes for modestly viewing risqué plays, with tiny mirrors on their outer sticks for spying, with compartments for perfume or secret messages, and even for concealing a dagger. There were telescope fans which conveniently contracted or elongated, mourning fans, fortune telling fans, autograph fans, children's fans and even tiny doll's fans. In 1879 "The Language of the Fan" was registered in the Patent Office at Washington. Held in certain positions, the fan conveyed messages.

Today, milady has put aside the fan. She no longer needs one to hide her blushes. Still, something remains in an old fan: a bit of history, a glimmer of romance, a certain fascination.

Ruth B. Field

Photograph opposite
ANTIQUE FANS
Gerald Koser

Overleaf
ST. JOHNSBURY, VERMONT
Richard W. Brown

Little Church in the Dell

There's a little country church
Nestled in a cosy dell,
Where the people all come flocking
When the sexton rings the bell.

High above the sacred altar,
Shines a painted window fair;
Here the image of the Saviour
Smiles down on the people there.

Here they sing the old, old-fashioned;
Here they swiftly kneel to pray;
And the rafters, old and seasoned,
Sometimes echo words they say.

Here they listen very humbly,
On each Sabbath morn and night,
To the Word so simply spoken,
How to follow in the Light.

Here the organ, old and mellow,
Sends out music wondrous sweet;
And they pause in friendly greeting
Ere the Sabbath is complete.

There's a little country church
Nestled in a cosy dell,
Where the people all come flocking
When the sexton rings the bell.

Helen Loomis Linham

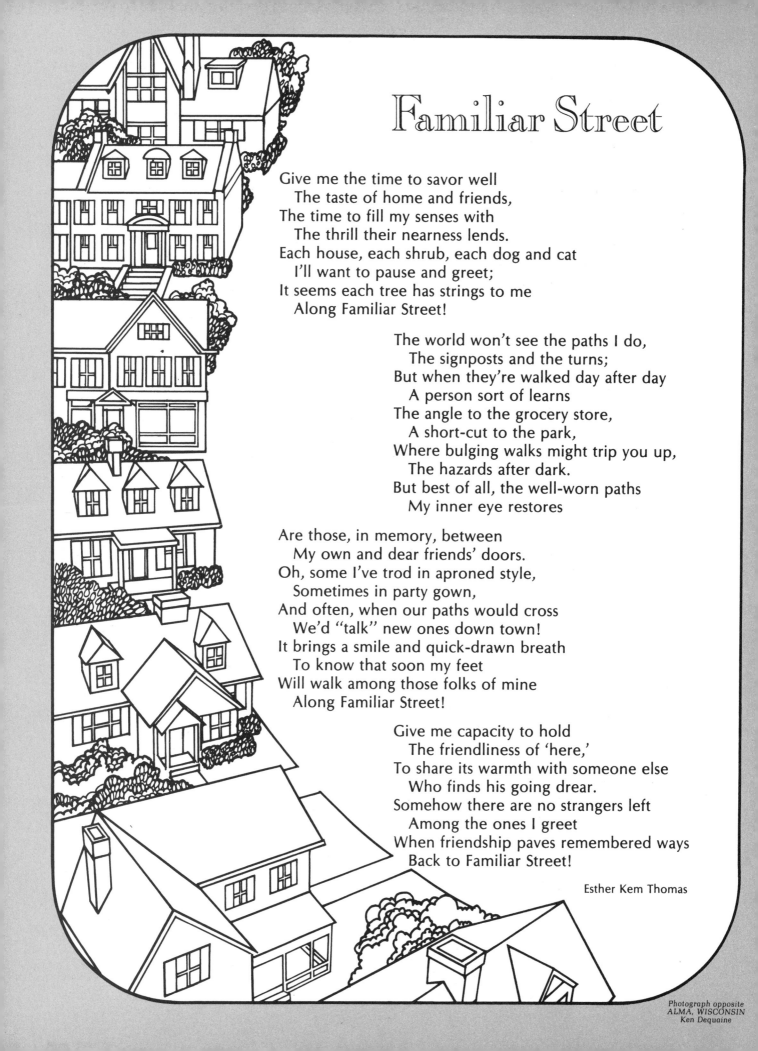

Familiar Street

Give me the time to savor well
   The taste of home and friends,
The time to fill my senses with
   The thrill their nearness lends.
Each house, each shrub, each dog and cat
   I'll want to pause and greet;
It seems each tree has strings to me
   Along Familiar Street!

      The world won't see the paths I do,
         The signposts and the turns;
      But when they're walked day after day
         A person sort of learns
      The angle to the grocery store,
         A short-cut to the park,
      Where bulging walks might trip you up,
         The hazards after dark.
      But best of all, the well-worn paths
         My inner eye restores

Are those, in memory, between
   My own and dear friends' doors.
Oh, some I've trod in aproned style,
   Sometimes in party gown,
And often, when our paths would cross
   We'd "talk" new ones down town!
It brings a smile and quick-drawn breath
   To know that soon my feet
Will walk among those folks of mine
   Along Familiar Street!

      Give me capacity to hold
         The friendliness of 'here,'
      To share its warmth with someone else
         Who finds his going drear.
      Somehow there are no strangers left
         Among the ones I greet
      When friendship paves remembered ways
         Back to Familiar Street!

Esther Kem Thomas

Photograph opposite
ALMA, WISCONSIN
Ken Dequaine

Buffalo Bill Cody

The life of Buffalo Bill Cody closely parallels the growth of the young western lands he loved and was such a part of. Born in Iowa in 1846, young Bill watched the wagon trains heading west, seeking land in Kansas and gold in California. Later, Cody also moved west to seek his fortune and, in the process, came to be identified by the whole world with a young and rugged land.

While he was still a youngster, William F. Cody was head of the family which included three sisters and his widowed mother. To support them, he signed on with a wagon train as its messenger. His salary was $40 a month; and in his spare time along the wagon route, he taught himself to read and write. The train went through Fort Laramie, a wild, western metropolis where the boy glimpsed lifelong heroes such as Jim Bridger and the incomparable Kit Carson. From that time on, Cody knew that he, too, would be a marksman and scout.

The young Bill's next steady job was with the Pony Express; but with the outbreak of the Civil War, he enlisted as a Union soldier. (Like his father before him, he was a strident abolitionist.) While serving as a hospital orderly, Cody met Louisa Frederici whom he married on March 6, 1866. At twenty years of age, the bridegroom sported the long, flowing locks of a scout and the flamboyant and fringed western garb.

After a brief, unsuccessful stint as an innkeeper, which he attempted mainly to please his wife, Cody signed on as a scout for General Custer. In the meantime, he also dabbled in real estate speculation, Indian fighting, and guiding eastern visitors looking for buffalo. One distinguished easterner who came west was James Gordon Bennett of the New York *Herald*. Bennett found Cody charming and carried tales back home of the wonderful scout. Another prestigious hunter for whom Bill served as guide was the Grand Duke Alexis of Russia. Out of gratitude to his guide, the Grand Duke awarded Bill a diamond-encrusted tie tack. Such recognition boosted Bill's growing reputation as the personification of the Wild West and earned him the nickname Buffalo Bill, which he used for the rest of his life. It is said that, while serving as a scout and a guide, Bill shot over 4,000 buffalo.

Capitalizing on Cody's growing fame, a man named Ned Buntline wrote a series of Buffalo Bill stories. One of them was dramatized and Bill went to the play's opening in New York. The rather melodramatic, overacted play was well received; but when the crowds spotted the actual Buffalo Bill in the audience, they went wild with applause. Thus, his new career, as one of America's most famous showmen, was launched.

Based on this inital success, Buntline conceived the idea of writing a play about Buffalo Bill, starring the real Cody. This play, *Scouts of the Plains*, was a smash hit. After a bout with stage fright, Bill, with his natural grace and innate acting ability, performed well. The show was as successful on tour as in New York City.

Bill's dream, however, was to stage a real extravaganza—a show as big as the west. He wanted to give eastern folks a taste of what life in the wild was like. At first, he advanced toward this goal by working animals and Indians into the shows. But, as his idea crystallized, it developed into a full-blown Wild West Show, with buffalo, Indians, great feats of horsemanship and marksmanship, and stars such as the incomparable Annie Oakley and Sitting Bull, chief of the tribe which vanquished Custer. "Buffalo Bill's Wild West Show" was the first of its kind; and it was such a success that it eventually toured the whole country and Europe.

On June 3, 1917, after a long and successful career with the show, Buffalo Bill died; and America lost one of her most original and colorful showmen. He is buried on Lookout Mountain north of Denver, overlooking the western land he loved.

Ellen Hohenfeldt

Those Street Vendors

The Ragman

"Rags, I say! Any rags today?"
  It was such a welcome sound.
The hooves clapped a beat
On the city street
  As the ragman drove around.

Soon the windows rattled open,
  Attic doors swung wide,
Then dozens of bags
Of old clothes and rags
  Appeared at the wagon's side.

"Rags, I say! Any rags today?"
  He sang as he moved along.
And the neighbors smiled,
For a little while,
  To hear the ragman's song.

The Vegetable Man

In horse and wagon days gone by,
  When the vegetable man drove round,
Fresh roasting ears
Or asparagus spears
  Showed up all over town.

Sometimes he brought green onions
  Or berries, red and sweet.
He'd weigh them all
And then he'd call
  His wares on every street.

"I have cherries! Fresh red cherries!"
  No shop along the mall
Can e'er replace
That friendly face
  Or sound the vendor's call.

Old-fashioned portraits by John Slobodnik

of Yesteryear

The Scissors Grinder

Remember the scissors grinder?
　　His bell had a special sound,
Like "a-RING-tee-tum!
It would really hum
　　As he pushed his cart around.

His honing wheel and whetstone
　　Made knives and scissors gleam.
Each sickle and blade
Were renewed by his trade
　　And mowers cut like a dream!

Remember the wheel and its turning,
　　Removing the rust and the strife,
With tales he would tell
And his grinder as well,
　　He brightened the pathways of life.

The Street Photographer

On certain sunny afternoons
　　Where children loved to play,
There'd come the beat
Of a pony's feet
　　Along the cobbled way.

The smiling, street photographer,
　　With his camera and his hood,
Sold pony rides
And prints besides
　　In each friendly neighborhood.

Unlike some passing fancies,
　　Replaced by fashion's rage—
His pony's gone,
His work lives on
　　In each family album page.

Poetry by Alice Leedy Mason

Summer Soliloquy

Summer's come on kitten feet;
Gentle breezes blowing
Like little kitten sighs.
Pensive cat, you are
So languid, still . . .
Revelling in the summer sun
As the world sings round you.

Happy bird sounds filter
Through lacy garments green—
Bees in quick, ambitious flight,
Their phantom wings abuzz,
Seek scented flowers bright.

Velvet pansies, alive, aglow,
Are little people faces
Nodding, bobbing,
Sharing summer secrets.

Azure skies, sailboat clouds
Drifting, billowing
In graceful harmony;
Soft as a butterfly's
Gossamer wings.

Stay, pensive cat,
Sink into summer.
Life is this honey-sweet day,
Tranquil and free,
Just right for dreaming.

Joan Callahan

Photograph opposite
Anne MacDonald

from the editor's scrapbook

To live is not to live
for one's self alone;
let us help one another.

Menander

Try to do to others as you would have them do to you, and do not be discouraged if they fail sometimes. It is much better that they should fail than that you should.

Charles Dickens

How beautiful a day can be
when kindness touches it.

Elliston

Just to work a little harder
For other people's good,
And to show a bit more friendship—
My friend, that's brotherhood.

Author Unknown

The best things are the simplest things: home and love and work to do, flowers in the garden, and bread from the generous fields. Lacking these, what else can make life worth the living? Having them, give thanks with joy; we need no more.

Author Unknown

A brave man inspires others to heroism, but his own courage is not diminished when it enters into other souls; it is stimulated and invigorated.

Washington Gladden

Loving kindness is greater than laws; and all the charities of life are more than all ceremonies.

Talmud

A light heart lives long.

Shakespeare

No thought is beautiful which is not just, and no thought can be just, that is not founded on truth.

Joseph Addison

So long as we love, we serve. So long as we are loved by others I would almost say we are indispensable; and no man is useless while he has a friend.

Robert Louis Stevenson

Yesterday's successes belong to yesterday with all yesterday's defeats and sorrows. The day is Here. The time is Now.

Elbert Hubbard

Flowers leave some of their fragrance in the hand that bestows them.

Chinese Proverb

Thou shalt love thy neighbor as thyself.

Mark 12:31

Our aim should be to do each day something worthy, some noble deed in kindness which brings joy and gladness to our fellowman, for this brings us a step nearer to God.

Unis

If a man does not make new acquaintances as he passes through life, he will soon find himself left alone. A man should keep his friendships in constant repair.

Johnson

Come out, come out across the hills! The golden blossoms call.

Sara Hamilton Birchall

A Country Lane

A country lane goes through my mind,
A lane that my heart runs back to find;
A lane where the air is cool as dew
And the ferns are high and the rocks are few,
And every branch of the tallest tree
Would whisper a fairy tale to me;
And every bird had a golden note
In the song that came from his crimson throat;
And life had a hundred gifts to give,
And I had a hundred years to live.
A country lane goes through my mind,
A lane that my heart runs back to find;
My heart, for never my feet will go
To walk that lane that I used to know,
For maybe my eyes would fail to see
The vision that memory holds for me,
And I'd miss the fairy tales I heard
And the song of the crimson-throated bird.
So I'll keep the dear unbroken spell
Of the country lane I love so well.

Nan Terrell Reed

Photograph opposite
Fred M. Dole

A Summer Creed

I believe in the flowers and their glorious indifference to the changes of the morrow.

I believe in the birds and their implicit trust in the loving Providence that feeds them.

I believe in the prayer-chanting brooks, as they murmur a sweet hope of finding the far-distant sea to which they patiently run.

I believe in the whispering winds, for they teach me to listen to the still, small voice within my feverish soul.

I believe in the vagrant clouds, as they remind me that life, like a summer day, must have some darkness to reveal its hidden meaning.

I believe in the soft-speaking rains, accented with warm tears, telling me that nothing will grow save it be fertilized with tears.

I believe in the golden hush of the sunsets, reflecting a momentary glory of that great world beyond my little horizon.

I believe in the holiness of twilight, as it gives me sense of the presence of God, and I know I am not alone. And whatever else I believe is enshrined in those abiding feelings that lie too deep for words.

W. W. Argow

The Old
Grist Mill

Many years the mill has stood,
groaning and creaking by the edge of the wood.
Silent phantoms dwell in this mill,
guarding the secrets of the hills.

The timbers, still strong over the years,
speak of labor, heartaches, joy and tears.
Memories linger in the corners—so still
preserved is the past of the old grist mill.

Silently the shadows cast their spell
touching our hearts by the stories they tell.
We remember our heritage is from the hills
as we stand quietly by the old grist mill.

Sharon Rose Davison

Photograph opposite
Fred Sieb

What Is a Dad?

A dad is a person you can always rely upon to be strong.

A dad is strength and steadiness. Like a sturdy oak he stands, sheltering his growing family from the storms and adverse winds of life.

A dad is the person who always knows that time is a great leveler. He has the patience, born of experience, that takes the long view and sees the sun shining beyond the present storm.

A dad is the person you go to when you know you will get a straight answer. He never glosses things over or coats them with sugar, but will always tell you the facts.

A dad is a person who always has a sage bit of wit or wisdom for any situation, drawn from the wealth of his experience and acquaintance.

A dad is the person who can turn a seeming calamity into a smile by turning the light side up.

A dad is the person who earns and deserves the title head of the house. It is his judgment and foresight that safely steers the home ship through the years.

A dad is a person who talks less about love than he shows it. His love is always there, evident in the dust in his face when he comes home at night, the sweat on his brow, and the strong hands that are continually working for his family.

A dad is the person who sets the example his children most want to emulate. His industry, devotion and care are the heritage his sons and daughters carry with them throughout their lives.

A dad is the reason that sons are proud to have sons who will proudly carry the name he has blessed.

A dad is the reason Father's Day is special. And it's because of dads like you!

Roger L. Kerr

To The June Bride

My dear, this is your wedding day
With dawn of goldenrod and blue
And clouds of pink and lavender
And necklace strung with pearls of dew.

This is your day adorned in lace
And gowned with gems reflecting light
And scarlet roses young and gay
To hold on arms of milky white.

This is your day with wishes born
In happy hopes both new and old
And of desires now fulfilled
And breathless beauty to enfold.

This is your day of prayers and vows,
Of tattered shoes and showered rice,
Of laughter and of quiet tears
And cake with figurines to slice.

This is your day to last for life,
From which to never draw apart,
A day of tinkling silver bells
To always echo in your heart.

John C. Metcalfe

June

I never remember in April how tall the grass will be in the pastures and hayfields by June. Or that daisies will frost the fence row and buttercups gild the meadow. I forget that choke-cherries will be in bloom with their sharp-tanged fragrance, and that June is other things than roses and honeysuckle.

June is really a time of relative quiet, serenity after the rush of sprouting and leafing and flowering and before the fierce heat that drives toward maturity and seed. June's air can be as sweet as the wild strawberries that will grace its middle weeks, sweet as clover, a sweetness that might be cloying if it weren't still so new.

Birds are still singing at their best, not only morning and evening but all through the day. The oriole, the tanager and the robin can make an early day vibrate with song, and a part of the song seemed this morning to be in the air even when I couldn't hear a bird note. The rasping that is July and August, the scraping of cicadas and all their kin, is yet in abeyance. June doesn't assault the ears. It flatters them and softens the call of the frog and the whippoorwill and is a joy.

These things I seem to have to learn all over again each June, and I wonder how I could have forgotten. I shall forget them again, and next March I shall think of June and roses and wonder what else it was that made last June so wonderful. Then June will come again and I shall find it a happy memory rediscovered and ready to live again.

Hal Borland

Vacation Days

Sing me a song of the out-of-doors,
Of the mountains, field and sea,
Where the skies are clear and the breezes cheer,
And the heart of man is free.

I am overspent by the ceaseless din
Of the subway and the street;
For the crowds distress and the walls oppress
With their sultry gathered heat.

Give me a glimpse of the meadows green,
Give me space where I can see;
I will roam at will and enjoy the thrill
Of creation's ecstasy.

Let me dream awhile as I hear the song
Of the robin, thrush and wren;
I shall find release in an inward peace
And return refreshed again.

Alfred Grant Walton

Queen Anne's Lace

Queen Anne's lace, a lovely flower,
Born of meadow, field, and bower.
Its pattern intricate and planned;
It shares its beauty with the land.

It's common, yes, though rare indeed,
Endowed by God it sows its seed.
"A weed," they say. "No weed," say I;
"Could weed so bless a summer sky?"

It bursts its blossoms on the scene,
Its petals white, on stems of green.
So lacy, delicate and fair,
Adopted by the summer's air.

Though not bold, it's not one bit shy;
It flirts with every butterfly.
It grows in crowds upon the hills,
And mingles with the daffodils.

So strange, it is by kings unseen
Though, ne'ertheless, named for a queen.
So many flowers are fair of face,
Yet none compare with Queen Anne's lace.

Dorothie R. Vickers

Life's Own Bouquet

I have not seen in their glorious array,
Flowers more resplendent than life's own bouquet!
Life's sweetest blossoms are often unseen,
Things we hold dearest of priceless esteem!

In friendship's garden with tender loving care,
You will find blossoms that are fragrant and rare.
When cultivated, they flourish and grow
In springtime and summer, in wintertime's snow.

Lilies of the valley soon wither and die,
They are trod underfoot and eventually passed by.
But flowers we gather in life's own bouquet
Grow fragrant and sweeter day after day!

Memories are precious and cherished indeed
Like lilacs in blossom, tenderly retrieved,
Embrace of a loved one, or a sweetheart's smile,
A child's rippling laughter, a maiden's sweet guile!

No beauty compares to the bud of a rose
Or the beautiful love that a mother bestows.
When the world is in turmoil, uncertain, unsure,
God's love is a refuge, a garden secure.

I have not seen in a floral display,
Flowers more resplendent than life's own bouquet!

Donita M. Dyer

LET'S BE FRIENDS— provides a deeper more meaningful understanding of the personal situations one encounters along life's road. In this delightful gift book of light, pleasurable reading, author Nat Olson cheerfully advises how to get along with people and how to find hope and trust in today's world. Hardcover— 7" x 9⅞"— 64 Pages— $3.50

THE SIMPLE JOYS— are what make life so special . . . the innocence of children, the majesty of a sunrise, the mysteries of the changing seasons. Reflect upon these many splendid wonders as portrayed in touching verse and full color photos. Hardcover— 7" x 9⅞"— 64 Pages— $3.75

TO ORDER: See order blank in back of this issue or write, Ideals Publishing Corporation, Dept. N-89, P.O. Box 1101, Milwaukee, WI 53201

Friendships

Many chance acquaintances are met from day to day. Many fall in step with us along life's winding way . . . But only one can ever bear the sacred name of friend—the one who with unfailing love keeps faith unto the end.

Time alone can prove the worth of friendships. Time's the test. As time goes by, we find we lose the false and keep the best . . . Friendship that is real and true and worthy of the name, changes not; through joy and sorrow, it remains the same.

Patience Strong

The Sundial

I record the shining hours—not the shadows and the showers . . . Only when the sky is blue—can I tell the time for you.

I ignore the clouds of grey—knowing they will pass away . . . From the dawn until the night—I declare that God is Light.

You who pass with downcast eyes —Look up at the golden skies . . . Mark the good hours, one by one—Turn your face towards the sun.

Patience Strong

Friendship

ISSUE

ideals

Ideals' Pages from the Past

On the following six pages, we are presenting a selection from Friendship Ideals 1951.

A Handshake

Orrin Alden De Mass

There's somethin' in a handshake
That's hard to just explain;
But it's mighty like the sunshine
That follows after rain.

*Like a friendly smile, that helps you
When roads are rough and long,
Like echoes through the shadows
Of cheery bits of song;*

Like the breezes soft of springtime
To green the hills of May,
Rest that comes with twilight,
At closing of the day.

*There's a heap of meaning hidden
In the clasping of the hands,
As if a heart was trying to say
It sort of understands.*

And oft a lonely soul takes hope
And seems to smile again.
There's somethin' in a handshake
That's hard to just explain.

Friends

Edgar Daniel Kramer

When I turn from my tasks at dusk,
  Though cold winds blow, though lilacs bloom,
I find him waiting at the gate
  To walk with me across the gloom,
And, entering a little house,
  We leave the world and all its woe,
The while we eat our meat and bread
  Within the lamplight's mellow glow.

His eyes as bright as twinkling stars,
  He hearkens, as the kettle croons,
And, supper done, he wants to help
  To put away the plates and spoons,
But laughingly I shake my head
  And say he is a clumsy elf,
And so he wisely watches me
  Place each thing on its proper shelf.

I tamp tobacco in my pipe,
  I settle in my easychair,
And, as he sits across from me,
  I know that life is strangely fair,
In spite of tears and shattered dreams,
  In spite of selfishness and lies,
For I am finding peace and strength
  Within the trust that fills his eyes.

Although we never say a word,
  The shadows and the drifting smoke
Are startled, as they hear us laugh
  Or chuckle at some silent joke,
For hearts, that truly understand
  Each other, in a nod, a sigh,
A look are speaking fluently,
  Just as we do, — my dog and I.

My Neighbor's Little Boy

Rosabel Boyd

Sturdy, boisterous, tiny lad
  of "just passed three"
Who, sometimes I must confess,
  lives far too near to me,
For often when I long for quiet,
  and noises do annoy,
Here comes the rattle-prattle
  of my neighbor's little boy.

I look out intending to wear
  a vicious frown,
Instead I feel reluctant smile
  come creepin' up and 'round,
For he eyes me with that nonchalance
  so companionable to boys,
As he jostles 'cross my terrace
  with his awkward load of toys.

Makes no difference when he sees me —
  if it's forty times a day,
He sends forth a cheery "hello"
  and comes racing o'er the way,
Or, he joins me in my garden
  as I find a quiet nook,
And sits by me, talking, talking,
  as I try to read my book.

Sturdy, boisterous, tiny lad
  of "just passed three",
I view you with compassion,
  for I understand, you see,
My boy is grown up now
  and no longer may annoy,
As he did once when he was called
  "my neighbor's little boy."

Ships

As I lie and watch the ships at sea
Waiting for one that is meant for me,
I think of the years and the dream ships past
And feel I shall know my ship at last.

As a child, my ship was a lovely thing,
Peopled with fairies who came to bring
A cargo replete with goodies and toys;
A ship just crowded with childish joys.

As I grew older, my ship changed, too;
The fairies were changed to a gallant crew
Who brought me friends and wealth untold.
All pleasures seemed mine with this load of gold.

Values change from childhood days,
Our ships change cargo in many ways.
But now I'm sure, as I watch the sea,
I want my ship to bring love to me.

Author Unknown

Summer

Summer's a great persuader
   Who makes a tarnished world bright.
Silent as time, this invader,
   Conquers the island of sight:
Patterns of green extending,
   Broken by patches of shore,
Rivers and lakes, unending,
   Where the dull and the dark were before.
Here, the green climbs a mountain;
   There, it nestles the corn.
Here it colors a fountain;
   There a valley is born.
This great green-crested invader
   Soon covers the sea and the sod.
For Summer's a great persuader
   That the earth is the handiwork of God.

Alice Leedy Mason

Coming in Countryside Ideals—

A charming excerpt from *Tom Sawyer* . . . Best-Loved Poet, Patience Strong . . . a special feature on "Plains, Georgia—Our President's Hometown" . . . Pages from the Past, Memory Ideals 1953 . . . plus poetry and pictures conveying the refreshing spirit of America's summertime landscape.

ACKNOWLEDGMENTS

SUMMER RAIN by William Arnette Wofford. From his book: A QUIET ROAD, copyright 1943 by William Arnette Wofford. Our sincere thanks to the following authors whose addresses we were unable to locate: John C. Metcalfe for TO THE JUNE BRIDE (original title: JUNE TWENTY-SIXTH) by John C. Metcalfe, Copyright 1963 by John C. Metcalfe; Nan Terrell Reed for A COUNTRY LANE (original title: A LITTLE GREEN LANE).

Additional photo credits: Front and back covers: Ralph Luedtke. Inside front cover: Ithaca, Wisconsin, Fred M. Dole. Inside back cover: Glacier National Park, Montana, Richard W. Brown.

COUNTRY SCENE SPECIAL OFFER!

We invite you to sample a healthy slice of country living through the pages of this beautiful publication. Each volume captures the essence of a season and provides interesting, entertaining and informative reading on a scale you never before have experienced. From helpful articles on home repair, gardening, sewing and cooking to timely and informative articles on ecology and travel, COUNTRY SCENE examines the broad scope of rural America and brings you information geared to living in and living with the wonderful land. In addition, there are many entertaining articles on bits and pieces of Americana ranging from the humorous and nostalgic to the historical and inspiring.

Each 80-page, soft-cover issue contains no fewer than 20 full-color illustrations reproduced on the finest glossy stock. A $2.50 value, each issue is yours for only $1.50—a savings of $1.00 per issue! This is a limited offer, so act now while supplies of each issue are available! Buy one, two, three or collect the entire set! We're sure the quality and beauty of this publication will please you.

FEATURE SECTIONS:

- What's Cooking—Country recipes
- Country Scenes—Poetry from our subscribers
- You Can Do It—Easy-to-make crafts and hobby projects
- Moving Right Along—Travel around America
- A Stitch in Time—Original sewing ideas
- The Environment—Using resources wisely
- The Country Craftsman—Rural craftsmen of today
- How Does Your Garden Grow?—Helpful gardening hints

Vol. 1, No. 1 Summer

Vol. 1, No. 2 Fall

Vol. 1, No. 3 Winter

Vol. 2, No. 1 Spring

Vol. 2, No. 2 Summer

Vol. 2, No. 3 Fall

Vol. 2, No. 4 Winter

Vol. 3, No. 1 Spring

**SPECIAL OFFER!
SAVE 40%**

★ *NO LONGER AVAILABLE BY SUBSCRIPTION*

JOIN OUR FAMILY OF DEDICATED READERS!

People have been buying IDEALS for nearly 35 years. Several generations of Americans have grown up with this unique publication until today IDEALS is known throughout the world for its dazzling color and its good taste in wholesome prose and poetry. We believe that this reputation is a great trust. That is why we continually strive to maintain this image by steadfastly choosing artwork and color photographs of only the highest quality. In many cases, our readers are our authors and poets. This is the way we want it! Because IDEALS is a magazine that is personally written and designed for our reader, each page is a personal message shared between our home and yours. We like it that way!

We would like you to join our family of dedicated readers. We invite you to share with us the peaceful beauty this world has to offer. Subscribe to IDEALS today! We're sure that it won't be long before we're fast friends. So sure, in fact, that we offer you this written pledge:

> *If, after receiving the first copy on your subscription, you find IDEALS MAGAZINE is not as beautiful and inspiring as you expected, just return your copy to us in its original wrapper marked "return to sender." We will cancel your subscription and the invoice due.*

So, act now! Enter a subscription today. And, don't forget those gift subscriptions! You needn't send any money now unless you prefer. Simply mark the proper area on the enclosed order blank or postage-paid order card and we'll bill you later.

Artwork and color photograph

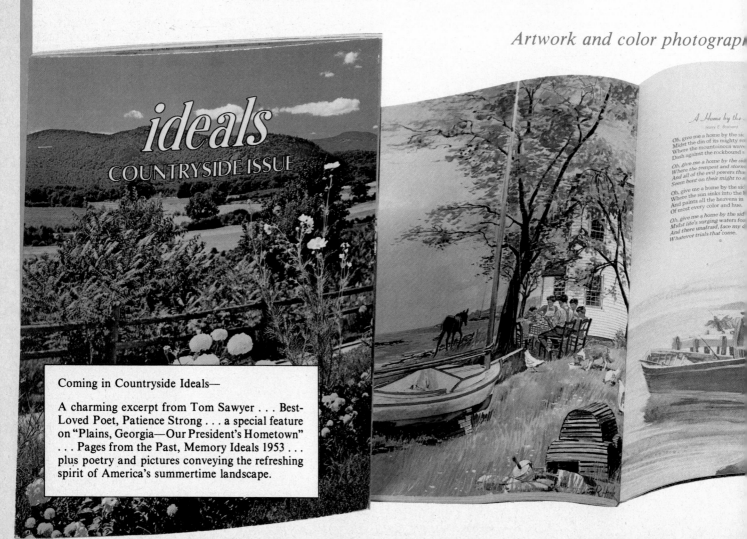

Coming in Countryside Ideals—

A charming excerpt from Tom Sawyer . . . Best-Loved Poet, Patience Strong . . . a special feature on "Plains, Georgia—Our President's Hometown" . . . Pages from the Past, Memory Ideals 1953 . . . plus poetry and pictures conveying the refreshing spirit of America's summertime landscape.

IDEALS Single Issues $2.50

IDEALS SUBSCRIPTION PLANS

ONE YEAR . . . 6 issues as published $10.00

    (Savings Value of $5.00 under the single copy rate.)

First Subscription	1-4 Additional	5 or More Additional
$10.00	$9.00 Each	$8.50 Each

TWO YEAR . . . 12 issues as published $17.00

    (Savings Value of $13.00 under the single copy rate.)

First Subscription	1-4 Additional	5 or More Additional
$17.00	$15.00 Each	$14.50 Each

1978
IDEALS PUBLICATION SCHEDULE

Fireside Ideals ....Jan.
Easter Ideals ....Mar.
Neighborly Ideals ....May
Countryside Ideals ....July
Thanksgiving Ideals ....Sept.
Christmas Ideals ....Nov.

f only the highest quality!

Six colorful issues
each year

Christmas Ideals 1944
"Our first Issue"

For 34 Years America's
Most Beautiful Magazine

Colorful Gift Books For All Occasions

Good books, like good friends, should be well chosen. Like friends, books should first prove reliable and trustworthy before they are made constant companions. Ideals Gift Books, because of their unfailing high quality and time-tested value, have proven faithful friends to their readers for more than 30 years. And like good friends, Ideals Gift Books are created to be shared with someone you love. Share one with a friend!

ORDER TODAY—SAVE 40%

The time to do so is now, because for a limited time only, Ideals Gift Books are priced amazingly low. Order today and SAVE 40% off the regular retail selling price. To order, see order area at the bottom of the enclosed order blank. Sorry, no substitutions.

. . . to Cherish	*. . . to Inspire*	*. . . to Share*
4 Book TOTAL VALUE $15.15 — NOW ONLY $9.00 GIFT SET A	5 Book TOTAL VALUE $19.75 — NOW ONLY $11.50 GIFT SET B	5 Book TOTAL VALUE $18.50 — NOW ONLY $11.00 GIFT SET C